Giving Effective Feedback

20 MINUTE MANAGER SERIES

Get up to speed fast on essential business skills. Whether you're looking for a crash course or a brief refresher, you'll find just what you need in HBR's 20-Minute Manager series—foundational reading for ambitious professionals and aspiring executives. Each book is a concise, practical primer, so you'll have time to brush up on a variety of key management topics.

Advice you can quickly read and apply, from the most trusted source in business.

Titles include:

Creating Business Plans

Delegating Work

Finance Basics

Getting Work Done

Giving Effective Feedback

Managing Projects

Managing Time

Managing Up

Presentations

Running Meetings

20 MINUTE MANAGER SERIES

Giving Effective Feedback

Check in regularly
Handle tough conversations
Bring out the best

HARVARD BUSINESS REVIEW PRESS

Boston, Massachusetts

Copyright 2014 Harvard Business School Publishing Corporation

Library of Congress Cataloging-in-Publication Data

Giving effective feedback : foster positive change, influence behavior, strengthen relationships.
    pages cm. — (20-minute manager series)
    Includes index.
    ISBN 978-1-62527-542-4 (alk. paper)
    1. Communication in personnel management.   2. Interpersonal communication.   3. Communication in management.   4. Supervision of employees.   5. Problem employees.   6. Feedback (Psychology)
    HF5549.5.C6G577 2014
    658.3'125—dc23

                                                    2014021082

ISBN: 9781625275424
eISBN: 9781625275479

Preview

As you interact with your colleagues, direct reports, and others within your organization, are you sharing feedback with them? Communicating in the right way with others about their actions can reinforce positive behavior and move them toward more productive courses of action—outcomes that benefit everyone. This book walks you through the basics of giving effective, results-oriented feedback so that it can become an integral part of how you work with others. You'll learn to:

- Recognize opportunities for giving feedback.

- Choose the best time and topics for discussion.

- Establish a rapport with others while giving them feedback.

- Ensure that your comments are valued.

- Prevent and manage volatile feedback situations.

- Create a work climate that encourages performance discussions.

Contents

Contents

Giving Effective Feedback

Why Feedback Matters

Why Feedback Matters

You've just received word that one of your direct reports, Judy, an IT help desk provider, was rude to a customer on the phone. You work well with Judy; she is one of your top performers and has never had a complaint filed against her. But the customer was very upset after the call. Is it worth raising the issue with Judy and risking your relationship with her?

Yes. Giving constructive feedback when it's needed is essential to creating a productive work environment—and it doesn't have to threaten your relationships. But you must give that feedback in the right way, so that the person receiving it can use what he hears from you to improve his own performance and that of his team and the organization.

Although the prospect of giving feedback often seems intimidating, it helps to remember that doing so is essential and, ultimately, beneficial. A feedback discussion is an opportunity for you to share your observations with others about their job performance to elicit productive change. In the example earlier, you want to explore with Judy what happened and make sure that her behavior isn't repeated—for the sake of her own development and for that of the organization.

Feedback is often corrective, which means it's intended to help the recipient change course or adjust practices when the current ones aren't working. It can also be positive, aimed at reinforcing good work and patterns of problem solving. Here's what you can accomplish by giving feedback:

- Show your direct reports and colleagues that you're attentive to them and their performance.

- Signal appreciation for a job well done.

- Redirect undesirable behavior.

- Point out a more productive course of action.

- Contribute to others' learning and development.

- Motivate and inspire individuals to higher levels of performance.

- Strengthen your rapport with coworkers.

- Foster open communication and enhance teamwork.

Delivering feedback should be a regular part of anyone's job, and it shouldn't be reserved for your direct reports. In select situations it can also be helpful to give feedback to a colleague or even a boss.

Consider the following example, in which constructive feedback is successfully communicated at an organization shortly after the testing of a new production process:

You've noticed that a bottleneck is occurring during a production phase overseen by your direct report Bill, who normally prides himself on his efficiency. After gathering the facts, you approach him to acknowledge the quality of his prior work and ask what he thinks is happening now. In discussing the situation, you discover that Bill has a misconception—namely, that the new production process requires more recordkeeping than the old one did. You clarify that the level of recordkeeping should remain the same and that it's only the format that has changed. As you and Bill look through his records together, you show him which elements he can omit, allowing him to save time and energy— and to return to his usual level of efficiency.

The feedback you give to Bill leads to a highly valuable change. By intervening early, you get durable results and also enable Bill to feel good about his work again. Feedback that people actually *hear* and *use* has this effect.

What makes feedback effective?

In order for your feedback to be heard and used, you need to deliver it at the right time and in the right way. To do that well, you need to understand what makes feedback most effective:

- It is shared frequently and in context.

- It aims to achieve a specific outcome.

- It is realistic in its expectations.

- It shows respect for the recipient.

- It is a two-way conversation.

- It is expressed as a point of view, rather than an absolute truth.

- It assumes an opportunity for follow-up.

These principles form the foundation of this book, which shows you how to give feedback effectively to improve the performance of your team and those around you. The first step, however, is overcoming your fear of giving feedback.

Overcome your fear of giving feedback

Even if in the abstract you know that giving feedback is valuable, you might still be hesitant to do it, especially when it comes to imparting corrective feedback. Some reasons for resistance include:

- You worry that giving feedback will make the recipient dislike you, or that it will strain your relationship.

- You assume that the other person cannot handle the feedback.

- You recall or know of previous instances when the recipient resisted feedback or didn't act on it.

- You feel that the person is already too stuck in his ways and that the feedback won't be helpful.

- You fear an awkward or even volatile situation.

In reality, though, fearing the worst will only close you off from productive conversations. Realizing that these hurdles are often self-constructed will help you clear them. So will sharing both positive and corrective feedback on a regular basis, as doing so will help you get used to having these types of conversations. Understanding the most effective way to prepare and handle a feedback discussion will help you overcome some of the issues that are holding you back.

Remember: Not only is giving feedback worth the risk of straining relationships, it is essential to the health of the organization.

Choosing When to Give Feedback

Choosing When to Give Feedback

P roviding feedback is not merely a hoop to jump through when the time for performance reviews rolls around. It should be an ongoing process woven into the fabric of everyday work. That's not to say that every behavior warrants input or a response. Feedback is most likely to have a positive, lasting effect when its focus is on behavior that the recipient is able to change and its delivery is well timed.

Identify the right situations

Offering feedback can be most useful in the following instances:

- When good work, successful projects, and resourceful behavior deserve to be recognized

- When the likelihood of improving a person's skills is high, because the opportunity to use those skills again is imminent

- When the person is already expecting feedback, either because a feedback session was scheduled in advance or because she knows that you observed the behavior

- When a problem cannot be ignored, because the person's behavior is negatively affecting a colleague, the team, or the organization

In other cases, feedback can be detrimental to the situation. Avoid giving feedback in these circumstances:

- When you do not have all the information about a given incident

- When the only feedback you can offer concerns factors that the recipient cannot easily change or control

- When the person who needs the feedback appears to be highly emotional or especially vulnerable immediately after a difficult event

- When you do not have the time or the patience to deliver the feedback in a calm and thorough manner

- When the feedback is based on your personal preference, not a need for more effective behavior

- When you have not yet formulated a possible
solution to help the feedback recipient move
forward

Bear in mind that when you give positive feedback
frequently, your negative feedback, when it is warranted, will seem more credible and less threatening.
Offering input only when problems arise may cause
people to see you as unappreciative or petty.

Perceptions of pettiness are especially likely if the
feedback recipient doubts your motives. Before you
deliver feedback, be honest with yourself about why
you want to give it. Sometimes you may be reacting to
your own needs and preferences, not what is best for
the team or organization.

For example, Sarah juggles more than one project
at a time, works late every night, and often rushes to
finish her work right before deadlines. She always
gets everything done—and does it well—but that kind
of schedule would stress you out. As Sarah's colleague,

you're inclined to reach out to her to give her corrective feedback on her time-management skills. But before you tell her that she's organizing her time poorly, first ask yourself whether her current time-management process actually diminishes the quality of her work. Sarah has always been good at collaborating with others, and her work has always been stellar. Perhaps she waits until the last minute because the added pressure helps her focus her energy toward a desired result. Perhaps she works late not because she doesn't have enough time in the day, but because it gives her the opportunity for quiet reflection after others have left the office.

In this case, your own work style and preferences may be driving you to give Sarah corrective feedback when it really isn't warranted. If Sarah detects that, she may be less likely to listen to necessary feedback that you offer in the future.

Can the behavior be changed?

Before choosing to give feedback, you need to understand whether the problem your colleague or direct report is facing is one that can be corrected. Figure 1 illustrates which behaviors and attributes tend to be easy to influence and which may be more difficult.

Feedback has the greatest impact on the first three items in the figure. You might focus on helping others with areas such as using a new database (job skills),

FIGURE 1

Influencing behavior: from easy to difficult

Easy to influence					Difficult to influence

Job skills	Time and work management	Knowledge	Attitudes	Habits	Personality traits

prioritizing tasks (time management), or learning a new tax code (knowledge).

Feedback is most likely to affect learning, growth, and change in areas that least threaten the recipient's sense of self-worth. Feedback about attitudes, habits, and personality traits can hit close to home. Does that mean you should not try to influence the behavior of a person who, for instance, wholly dislikes collaboration? Of course not. But it will be more effective to direct your efforts toward, say, getting that person to follow clearly outlined steps in a collaboration protocol rather than making a blanket demand that she "learn to enjoy teamwork." In other words, frame the request as a change in specific tasks or behaviors, rather than a personality makeover. If the person receiving the feedback sees your target as one that is beyond her control, or beyond your purview, she is likely to either dig in her heels and ignore you or direct her frustration inward and lose motivation.

Time the feedback

Once it's clear that feedback is the right route to take, identify the best time to sit down with your direct report or colleague. It's important to give feedback soon after you observe a behavior you want to discuss. It may be tempting to hold off to see if the behavior occurs again—or just because giving feedback can be hard to do—but you and the recipient will communicate most effectively about the situation when it is fresh in your minds. Waiting for a direct report's scheduled performance evaluation is typically too late to discuss the matter, as that could be months away. (See the sidebar "Distinguishing between feedback, coaching, and performance appraisals.")

Think again about Bill's situation with the production bottleneck. If Bill had not received feedback quickly, his struggle to keep up might have led to a missed client deadline, thereby compromising a revenue stream and lowering the entire production team's morale. His frustration would also have persisted, and, as his manager, you would have missed an opportunity to show him that you know he's capable of better work—something that goes a long way toward building rapport and self-motivation. People tend to have good associations with those who help them nip stress in the bud. If you had waited a long time to empower Bill to fix his problem, however, he might have been less receptive to the feedback when it finally came.

That said, feedback that is given too soon—in an impromptu manner with little or no forethought—can also be counterproductive. There is particular risk in quick assessments if the recipient feels you are overreacting or perceives you as insincere. Snap judgments ("Why on earth did you do that?") are demoralizing, and empty praise (a routine "Looks good") can be disappointing. Always gather the necessary facts and information before offering your perspective.

Now think back to Judy, your direct report who upset the customer during a phone call. You might need

DISTINGUISHING BETWEEN FEEDBACK, COACHING, AND PERFORMANCE APPRAISALS

If you determine that someone simply must change his attitudes or habits in order to perform well, one feedback discussion alone may not be enough. If the person is your direct report, you may need to craft a longer-term solution. One possibility is coaching, in which you'd develop a plan and a regular schedule for discussing feedback and engaging in other learning activities.

The results of both feedback and coaching can also be discussed in the context of a direct report's regular performance evaluation, which is distinct from routine feedback in its formality and its emphasis on past work. Performance evaluations are generally scheduled to occur at specific time intervals mandated by your organization, such as once or twice a year. See table 1 for a comparison of feedback, coaching, and performance appraisals.

(continued)

TABLE 1

Comparison of feedback, coaching, and performance appraisals

	Feedback	Coaching	Performance appraisals
Purpose	To reinforce or change behavior	To improve skills	To evaluate past work
Participants	Any two (or more) people	Usually supervisor to direct report, but can be multidirectional	Supervisor to direct report
Place	Private and quiet space	Depends on the skill to be learned	Usually in the supervisor's office
Tone	Typically casual, although can be more formal	Somewhat formal	Very formal
Timing	Frequent and as needed, or during formal sessions	Regular meetings	Prespecified junctures, such as every six months or every year
Follow-up	Continual	Continual	Based on an action plan

to listen to a recording of the call with the customer, review any pertinent records or transactions, and talk with other employees who witnessed the event to get the full story before talking to Judy directly.

If an incident was particularly upsetting, choose a time after both you and the recipient have had the opportunity to calm down and reflect on what happened. With the appropriate information in hand, you'll be able to respond thoughtfully when the time is right.

Finally, choose a time to provide feedback when the recipient can give you his undivided attention. Engaging someone on a Friday afternoon, just before a meeting, or on an especially busy day is likely to be unproductive. When offering feedback, context matters as much as content.

After you've identified the behavior to target and decided when you will approach the recipient of your feedback, it's time to plan and execute on the interaction itself. We'll cover this in the next chapter.

Conducting a Feedback Discussion

Conducting a Feedback Discussion

The goal of a feedback conversation is to reinforce positive behavior or improve performance. When giving corrective feedback in particular, don't just air your grievances or criticize; focus on the future by conveying the specific changes you want the person to make. That starts with careful planning.

Plan the interaction

No matter how quickly you need to give feedback to an employee, it's essential to prepare for the encounter.

Once you've determined that you need to share your perspective and decided when it needs to happen, shift to working on the substance of your feedback. Here's what you should consider:

- Gather all the information available about the behavior in question and its effect on the team or project to obtain an objective view of the issue. As you prepare, ask yourself what you would do if the recipient were to object to what you understand to be the facts, or if she presented other evidence you did not know about.

- Create a discussion plan. Jot down what you want to talk about, and anticipate the recipient's reactions to the feedback session. Craft some follow-up responses.

- Prepare yourself to listen, not just talk. You might, for example, allow for half of the session to involve asking the recipient questions and half to be spent listening to her answers, rather than making comments yourself. Also anticipate what kinds of questions she might have and expect to answer them.

- Consider what you want to get out of the discussion, both in the short term and the long term. (We'll discuss this in more detail in the upcoming chapter "Developing an Action Plan.")

Organize your thoughts in writing. Table 2, "Planning a feedback session," uses the example of Judy to show you how to identify the kinds of questions you will want to answer before you begin the discussion.

Then consider the logistics of your feedback session:

- Whenever possible, give the recipient advance notice that you want to speak with her regarding some performance feedback. Find

TABLE 2

Planning a feedback session

Points to prepare	Example
One-line overview	Judy was rude when a customer called the IT help desk.
Objective report of the behavior	The customer reported that Judy "spoke in a sharp tone of voice" and said that she had "no earthly idea" how long the server would be down. The customer said that when he asked for a rough estimate, Judy shouted at him.
Objective report of the effect on the team or project	Other help desk providers who overheard Judy's comments were distressed about them. The customer then complained, putting the reputation of the department—and the company—at risk.
Potential objections to the objective report and how you'll address them	Judy may deny that she spoke rudely. If she does, point out that the customer's and other help desk providers' reports corroborate one another. Share with her your understanding of what qualifies as rudeness.
Discussion plan	1. Give Judy the facts and show that you are aware of what has happened. 2. Listen to Judy's version of events. 3. Make clear that rude behavior to customers will not be tolerated. 4. Brainstorm with Judy about ways to avoid frustrating moments in the future.

Possible barriers to the feedback	Judy may be angry and anxious. She may not want to discuss what happened. She might defend herself rather than try to describe events accurately.
Ways to overcome the barriers	Don't be judgmental; hear Judy's side of the story. Give her your undivided attention, and be willing to listen if she has feedback for you.
What questions do you have?	What happened from Judy's point of view? How can she avoid losing control when frustrating moments occur in the future?
What questions might you be asked?	Judy may want to know more about what sort of behavior qualifies as rudeness. She might want to know what she is supposed to do if a customer asks about an IT matter she doesn't know the answer to. She may ask what she is supposed to do to improve her performance in the future.
Desired short-term result(s)	Have Judy commit to showing more respectful behavior toward customers immediately.
Desired long-term result(s)	Find a way to make the conditions of Judy's job less frustrating for her.

a time that she will find convenient, but without undue delay. Arrange to hold the discussion in private, particularly if the feedback is corrective.

- Arrange to have note-taking and scheduling tools at your disposal to record important points during the meeting as they're discussed. Having a pen, paper, and your electronic calendar at the ready shows that you intend to follow up.

A feedback recipient is much more likely to hear what you have to say and learn from the experience if she sees that you're prepared. You'll also be more relaxed as you communicate, and the recipient will feel more confident in accepting your guidance.

Initiate the exchange

The first few moments of any feedback session are crucial. The initial signals a feedback recipient perceives from you are likely to influence her attitude throughout the rest of the conversation.

When you're giving positive feedback, sending good early signals is usually not difficult. The very context—that you want to say something complimentary—is often enough. Identify what you're praising in specific terms. For example, "Maria, you did a great job on the Simmons project this past week. I was particularly impressed with how you handled the client's concerns about deadlines and the action plan you developed in response. I'd like to show what you did to the rest of the team." Don't end there. Ask Maria what allowed her to do such a great job. You may discover gems you didn't anticipate.

Corrective feedback can be more difficult. There is no foolproof formula, as individual circumstances and personalities will determine the best course of action. But these principles can help:

- Sit without physical obstacles, such as tables or desks, between you.

- Avoid interruptions. Silence your phone if you can, and ignore e-mail, texts, and other intrusions during the conversation. Focus completely on the person you're speaking with.

- Adapt your communication style to that of the recipient. For example, if she's a very social person, spend a few minutes talking casually before starting the feedback session in earnest.

- Assume a tone close to that of an experienced teacher: Show confidence in the guidance you provide, but don't be patronizing or judgmental in offering it.

- Consider the recipient's point of view and perspective. Try to understand who she is and how she wants to grow.

- Imagine yourself in the other person's shoes. Consider what you would need to hear in order to walk away from the conversation feeling ready for positive change.

- Be sensitive to ways in which gender, race, age, or other differences might affect the recipient's response to your feedback. Individuals with certain backgrounds, for example, might find direct, to-the-point feedback demotivating. In such cases a gentler discussion may be warranted.

Let's return to the example with Judy. You might be tempted to begin the conversation by summarizing what you've heard and laying down the law: "Judy, I've heard from a customer that you were really rude to him last week, and a number of other team members overheard and agreed. You just can't speak that way to a customer. What do you have to say for yourself?" This sort of approach is likely to make Judy defensive and isn't going to make her any less angry and anxious than she may already be (as you will have identified in your prep work).

Instead, you might start the conversation in the following way to remove some of the barriers you identified: "Judy, you know we're here to discuss what happened on your customer call earlier this week. I'd first like to share the information I have about the situation, and then I want to hear your point of view. After that, we can discuss what to do next. How does that sound to you?" Because you opened the discussion in this way, Judy can immediately see it as a two-sided conversation and understand that you aim to work with her to find the right solution to the problem. She'll know that she will have a chance to be heard, and that may make her feel less angry and anxious and more respected. You can then describe your understanding of the incident and encourage her to share her point of view.

Engage in dialogue

Whether you are giving positive or corrective feedback, once you have initiated the conversation and have described the issue to the recipient effectively, encourage her to explain her behavior in her own words. Pay close attention to how she responds. Specifically, you should do the following:

- *Listen actively.* Concentrate on the recipient's message and its implications rather than on your response. In particular, listen to what she is describing and what images and metaphors she uses, and if you don't understand something, ask.

- *Notice nonverbal cues.* Take note of the recipient's body language and tone. Does her tone of voice and facial expression match what she's saying? Does her body language appear tense or uncomfortable? Comment on what you see and ask her to tell you more about it. ("Judy, you seem angry. Did something I said seem unfair to you? Tell me about it.")

- *Monitor your own reactions.* Sitting back and crossing your arms both imply resistance.

Tapping your pencil or eyeing your smartphone suggest you're not interested. If you lean forward, maintain eye contact, and nod your head, you show that you're listening and understanding what the other person is saying. The feedback recipient may also use this opportunity to give *you* feedback—you need to handle that with the same openness you expect of her (see the sidebar "Receive feedback openly.")

- *Paraphrase what the recipient says.* By restating her response in different words, you show the other person that you have understood her point. If anything is unclear, ask more questions until both of you are on the same page.

In cases of corrective feedback, after you share your concerns and listen to the recipient's point of view, you'll want to identify the core issue at play. That's not always as easy as it seems; sometimes surface behavior stems from a deeper problem.

RECEIVE FEEDBACK OPENLY

As you talk about an issue, listen to the recipient, and ask questions, you may discover that he has feedback for *you* about a particular process, how you communicate, or how you've interpreted the issue at hand. You must learn how to receive feedback openly—and to value its rewards.

When others give you honest feedback, you have an opportunity to improve your relationships with them by showing how well you interact with people, your awareness of the impact of your own behavior and actions on others, and your process for getting work done. Here are some tips to remember as you receive feedback:

- Listen carefully to the other person's point of view, and consider the feedback giver's intention. What does he want you to take away from

(*continued*)

RECEIVE FEEDBACK OPENLY

this discussion? Think about the validity of the feedback, and ask questions if you're unclear about anything that's been said.

- Let your defenses down. If you find yourself getting upset, try breathing deeply or taking a short break.

- Resist the urge to justify the behavior or actions that are being criticized. Wait for your chance to respond, and present your perspective clearly and calmly.

- Identify what you can learn from the feedback. Focus on how you can improve in the future and how the person giving the feedback may be able to help with that effort.

- Come up with a plan of action. Work with the person giving the feedback to develop a series of steps you can take, and ask for his support. Write down your plan as you discuss it.

- Finally, recognize when criticism of your behavior, even when valid, has no place in the current conversation. If that is the case, set aside a separate time to discuss that feedback, and continue with the issue at hand.

You always have the right to verify feedback you've received with other sources of information. This can help validate or modify the message you've been given. But always thank the other person for the feedback: It is a gift that can improve your relationship.

If, for example, you have an employee who is regularly late to work, you may both agree that's the problem that needs to be solved. But the underlying causes may not be evident. She may be late to work because she's having difficulties at home, or she may be unhappy about work and resisting coming into the office. She may simply be unconcerned about her precise arrival time, because she consistently gets her work done in a timely manner. Digging down to the root cause will allow you to analyze next steps that can correct the behavior and help the recipient—and the rest of the team—work more productively.

There is no easy script to follow for feedback discussions. Every conversation is different based on the situation and the people involved. But following the steps presented in this chapter will give you the best chance at having a fruitful conversation. In the next chapter, we'll help you turn a feedback discussion into practical steps by developing a plan of action.

Developing an Action Plan

Developing an Action Plan

S haring feedback—particularly corrective feedback—can be difficult, and many people breathe a sigh of relief when that step is done. But you're not finished yet. For feedback to be truly effective, it has to be heard *and* implemented. The next step of the process is planning how to move forward.

Specify next steps

For positive feedback, consider sharing the person's good work with others as an example or asking her to train or coach her colleagues on an area she's excelled in. It's easy to overlook such valuable opportunities when you're in the thick of daily work, but sharing the key to one employee's success may increase others' efficiency and motivation.

For corrective feedback, after you and your direct report or colleague have identified the core issue that needs to be addressed, work together to develop an action plan for moving forward that is mindful of the root cause of the behavior. If, for example, you have discovered that your employee is always late to work because she has a long commute, you may be able to offer her the flexibility to work from home a few days each week. You can also emphasize the effect her behavior is having on others as added incentive to help her change her ways: If she discovers that her behavior is lowering the morale of those who are punctual in addition to affecting her individual productivity, she may be more motivated to arrive on time. Here are other options to consider:

- *Offer a carrot.* Find more interesting and satisfying assignments for the employee to work on as an incentive to arrive on time.

- *Use a stick.* Require that she be prompt, and establish explicit consequences for tardiness (for example, documenting the situation in a formal performance review, which could later hamper her chances for promotion).

- *Seek an alternative.* Explore the possibility of formally changing her hours so she can come in an hour later and work an hour later each day, or work from home one or more days per week. You might even institute a flexible schedule for the entire group so that everyone has the option of arriving at work within a range of times.

Whichever approach you take, confirm that you and the recipient are leaving the feedback session with the same understanding of what will come next. Therefore, you should:

- Summarize the plan. If there are multiple components, specify each one.

- Have the recipient show that she knows what the next steps are. She might demonstrate her understanding by restating them or by agreeing to something you have written down.

- Explicitly ask how she feels about the plan. If any points seem unresolved, be open to clarifying them or, if appropriate, revising them.

- Identify when and how follow-up will occur. Be as specific as possible.

- Set a time frame for achieving the primary goal and, if appropriate, smaller goals along the way.

When specifying next steps, make sure that you and the recipient feel that the plan belongs to both of you. A sense of mutual ownership greatly increases the likelihood that the recipient will apply your feedback.

Follow up

For the sake of the employee, your team, and the organization, don't stop the process of change when the feedback session ends. After giving positive feedback, for example, continue to reinforce the good behavior. When others can learn from that behavior, follow up to arrange training or coaching sessions led by the individual you've praised.

In cases of corrective feedback, continue to observe how the employee is doing and whether she is following the agreed-upon action plan. Specifically, you should:

- Check in regularly to ensure that the action plan is on track. Follow the schedule you outlined as closely as possible.

- Ask the employee to describe her progress. Encourage her to be frank about any obstacles

she may be encountering, and do what you can
to help remove them.

- Be explicit about any improvements that you're
  noticing. Offer praise and reinforcement to
  bolster that progress.

- Be frank if you notice that progress has been
  too slow or is not happening at all. Discuss specific options for getting the situation on track.

Feedback is not a cure-all for workplace ills. In
some cases, you may discover that the feedback recipient just isn't changing his behavior, even after
multiple feedback sessions. There are many reasons
why this may happen: The employee disagrees with
you, doesn't understand the need for change, or just
doesn't care. If a problem persists despite vigilant
and judicious follow-up, you may have to take addi-
tional—and in some cases, more severe—measures.

If things aren't improving, consider whether there's
anything you might be doing to add to the problem.

Were you clear enough when you gave your feedback? Did the recipient understand what he should be doing, and are you supporting him? Ask for help and advice from human resources, or, if you're not the person's manager, consider reaching out to his boss for assistance. If the behavior (or lack thereof) continues, set up another feedback session, but include another person in the discussion as a witness, such as an HR representative. Document carefully what the person says and agrees to, as well as how he behaves and misbehaves. If there is no improvement, that person might not be the right fit for your team or organization.

If you have followed these steps and things progress to the point of termination, you'll know that you're doing the best thing for everyone involved. You, your team, and your organization do not need to suffer because of one person's behavior.

For more guidance on how to proceed if the recipient doesn't react well to your feedback, see "Handling Difficult Feedback Situations" later in this book.

Assess yourself

Don't forget your own role in the process. You, too, should be learning from feedback discussions. After a feedback session, use table 3, "Evaluating the feed-

TABLE 3

Evaluating the feedback process

Topic	What worked?	What could be improved?
PROCESS		
Planning the feedback		
Initiating the meeting		
Discussing pertinent points		
Listening to the recipient		
Developing an action plan		
RELATIONSHIP		
Communication style		
Recipient's reaction		
Level of mutual trust and respect		
RESULTS		
Impact of changes		
Timeliness of changes		
Expectations and progress		

back process," to evaluate how the meeting went, and monitor how follow-up is progressing.

Action plans, deliberate follow-up, and self-evaluation all reinforce the ongoing nature of con-structive feedback. In short, the learning (for your colleague *and* for you) doesn't end after the door on the feedback session closes. When you act with that principle in mind, your example has an impact on your colleagues and direct reports, and everyone on the team benefits.

Handling Difficult Feedback Situations

Handling Difficult Feedback Situations

I n most cases giving feedback proceeds smoothly and ends positively, even if the feedback is corrective. Sometimes, though, the situation may be more complicated. This chapter focuses on common feedback scenarios that present special challenges.

Dealing with noncommunicators

Some people are unresponsive when confronted with feedback, even when it is positive. The reasons for this may vary from a simple fear of not being liked, to preconceived notions about the person delivering the feedback, to cultural expectations about how to respond to authority. Whatever the reason, you must still handle the present situation directly, even if it makes the person uncomfortable.

When you need to give feedback to a quiet, shy, or otherwise uncommunicative person, patience is key. Don't rush the discussion, and don't try to force him to respond. Take deliberate pauses so the recipient has the chance to gather his thoughts and articulate them. Giving him enough space to think and speak can go a long way.

As you proceed, make an effort to draw out the other person's point of view. Ask open-ended questions, such as "What was your rationale for telling the customer we couldn't help him?" or "How did you prepare for the presentation?" that require more than a yes or no response. These types of questions, which are useful in any feedback situation, show an uncommunicative person that you want to hear and understand his point of view. In effect, you're saying, "My version of the issue is not the only one."

Managing potentially volatile encounters

In contrast with noncommunicators, some corrective feedback recipients may be openly defensive as soon as they're confronted with criticism. That defensiveness may stem from the recipient's desire to convey his understanding of the facts. As part of your process (as described in "Conducting a Feedback Discussion" earlier in this book), you'll encourage him to share his point of view, and you should always be willing to acknowledge when you have the facts wrong.

More often, however, defensiveness surfaces because productive and honest communication is breaking down, leading the recipient to misperceive your motives and intentions.

Think back to the first chapter of this book, and imagine a different version of the scenario involving Bill, the usually efficient worker who is causing a bottleneck in a new production run. This time, when you outline the problem for Bill, he blows up, saying, "Why did you wait so long to tell me about this? I've got a new system now, and it's too late to change it. Not to mention all those extra nights I've been working!" When you try to explain that you have only just heard about the issue, Bill says it's time for his break and walks out of your office.

Volatile encounters like this one can be hard to defuse once they've begun. If you anticipate that your feedback session could become contentious, plan ahead:

- If the employee is already upset or angry, wait until he calms down before you engage him directly. (Keep in mind, though, that even when surface emotions seem smooth before the feedback session, unsettled feelings can always bubble up, sometimes right before you meet with the person or during the encounter itself.)

- Write down your feedback points in advance so you won't get distracted and forget them during the session.

- Plan and rehearse how you will respond to outbursts before you initiate a conversation with the recipient. (Table 2, "Planning a feedback session," which appears earlier in this book, can be particularly helpful in preparing you for potentially difficult interactions.)

- Plan to keep your feedback simple; limit yourself to one or two primary points. Volatile situations can be made worse when you catalog what the feedback recipient may perceive as a long list of grievances.

Once you are in the session with the recipient:

- Elicit the recipient's point of view and actively listen to his response to avoid confrontations during the discussion.

- Soften his defensive posture with phrases that show him that he's being heard, such as "I hear what you're telling me" or "That's an important perspective." In addition, note points of agreement between you to establish common ground. Comments like "You and I are on the same page about that" help to convey that you want to work with—rather than against—the other person.

- Remain composed. Speak slowly, calmly, and clearly. Avoid phrasing that might be interpreted as judgmental. For example, "Can you help me understand that point a bit better?" is much less confrontational than "I have no idea what you mean."

- Redirect his focus away from the point of dissension. Work on building small agreements about basic details: what happened, when, and so on.

In the case of Bill, you might start the conversation not by outlining the problem with the production run but by asking him to share how he thinks the new run is going. That would give Bill the chance to identify the problem before you do. If Bill does not volunteer the information, make clear that you have only just learned about the matter before describing it in detail: "Bill, I just learned about a blip in our production run, and, given your knack for efficiency, I wanted to get your insights first." That approach will signal to Bill that you trust him and appreciate his work—and assure him that you haven't been sitting on information for a long time before consulting him. And, of course, rehearsing that line before you meet with Bill will help you deliver it in a neutral, nonjudgmental tone.

If Bill still becomes defensive despite these efforts, focus on details or facts about the production run that are objective and that you both agree upon: "Yes, you're correct that the new run lasts three days." You will eventually get to the nub of the problem, but if you have established common ground first, you will be less likely to face a scenario in which Bill feels the need to storm out of your office.

Giving feedback to high performers

Sometimes the toughest people to influence with feedback are those who do the best work. But giving stars effective feedback is essential to keeping them engaged and motivated—and to helping them reach their potential. Experts make clear that you should not bend the basic principles of giving feedback when dealing with top performers: No matter who is receiving the feedback, the advice in this book applies. But here are a few tips that can extend those basics to the unique needs of top performers:

- *Express gratitude for current performance.* A star may not know how well she is doing. Always start your feedback session with a top performer by stating what she has accomplished and thanking her for it.

- *Understand the cost of great results.* It's important to understand *how* top performers have achieved their exemplary outcomes, and at what cost. For example, did she forgo other things, such as caring for her team, building alliances with others, or maintaining a healthy work-life balance in order to accomplish her goals?

- *Don't assume the star is perfect.* Everyone can improve, and you do a top performer a disservice if you fail to help her grow—particularly if you're her manager. Focus on what comes next in her career, and identify which obstacles might be standing in her way and how she can overcome them.

- *Find out how you are doing.* Ask questions such as "How can I continue to support your high performance?" or "What can we do as an organization to keep getting better and supporting your great work?" By asking these questions, you'll encourage this key player to see you as an ally in her development.

The better the performer, the more often she needs feedback. You and your organization depend on retaining top performers, so it is a wise investment of your time and energy to support and develop them. Giving them regular positive reinforcement and turning their attention to self-improvement allows your stars to celebrate success and work effectively toward what comes next.

Giving corrective feedback to your boss

As we've discussed, providing feedback to a direct report or a colleague can be delicate. Even trickier is giving corrective feedback to your boss. In these instances, a good rule of thumb is to tread lightly. A few tips can help:

- *Identify the issue.* Start by discussing the problem with your team members. Is this something that others are struggling with as well?

- *Decide whether the matter is worth pursuing.* Consider alternatives. If you and other members of your team can minimize the impact of your manager's behavior on your own, you may not need to approach her at all.

- *Prepare carefully.* If you must give your manager corrective feedback, collect objective data such as e-mails, job descriptions, events, dates, and so on. But present them as aids in finding a solution, not as an arsenal of evidence.

- *Make an appointment.* Don't surprise your manager. Let her know that you want to discuss an important issue with her privately. Ask for a particular time and place to meet.

- *Describe the behavior and its impact on the team.* Give the feedback directly, accurately, and above all, respectfully. Describe the behavior you're targeting, not a personality trait. Avoid an accusatory tone of voice.

- *Make a suggestion or a request, not a demand.* Eventually, move from a statement of the problem to a possible resolution. You will know whether your manager is ready to meet this challenge. If so, she may join you in considering various options for improving the situation.

- *Check for commitment to change.* Even if the process goes well, make sure you are both clear about the next steps. Ask something like, "So do we agree on how we'll adjust the process for the team moving forward?" Show your willingness to do your part.

Giving corrective feedback to your boss is a relatively rare event, as are feedback situations that escalate to a crisis level. The best way to prevent the most difficult feedback situations from ever occurring is to create an overall work climate that encourages and welcomes feedback. We'll discuss that next.

Creating a Receptive Climate for Feedback

Creating a Receptive Climate for Feedback

F eedback is most likely to be accepted and lead to positive change when the recipient believes that the person giving it is reliable and has good intentions. As a leader, creating a general climate that encourages feedback is the most effective way to help all those who give feedback in your workplace—yourself included—earn that kind of trust.

Make feedback a priority

Frame feedback—positive or corrective—as an ongoing process, not an occasional and arbitrary comment or correction. Make sure everyone around you knows that giving and receiving feedback is an ongoing goal with the intention of improving the entire organization. Let the managers you oversee know that if they treat giving feedback as a mere requirement to complete at the time of performance reviews, they will not meet one of *your* basic expectations. A useful mantra is "Every single day, the people you work with and those who work for you should know how they're doing."

To show others that feedback is a large part of your organization's or your team's culture, you need to set an example and give feedback regularly and visibly. Do this not only in your individual feedback discussions but in your day-to-day actions as well. Be as open to receiving feedback from your colleagues, including your direct reports, as you are to sharing your observations of their work. Don't just sit back and wait for feedback to be offered, particularly if you're in a leadership role.

Give positive feedback publicly

Acknowledging positive performance frequently and publicly is a good way to start building a culture of frequent feedback. And don't just do it yourself: State explicitly that you expect everyone else on your team to follow suit.

Embracing positive feedback and acknowledging good work promotes personal development and shows others that feedback doesn't need to cause anxiety. By regularly acknowledging good work, your direct reports and colleagues will trust your message and be more open to your corrective feedback when it's necessary.

When you give positive feedback as part of building this kind of culture, follow these guidelines:

- *Start small.* Don't assume that only big wins merit discussion. When you see *any* behavior you want to encourage, acknowledge it and express appreciation. Make clear to direct reports and colleagues that it matters even when the little things are done well.

- *Praise effort, not ability.* Take a cue from research by Stanford psychologist Carol Dweck: Her work suggests that praising persistent efforts, even in failed attempts, helps build resilience and determination, whereas praising talent and ability results in risk aversion and heightened sensitivity to setbacks. A work climate that values effort, therefore, can increase ability.

- *Offer some positive feedback—and stop there.* Using positive feedback only to cushion the blow before delivering criticism will degrade the value of your praise and render it hollow. Sometimes reinforcing good work is enough. Set a tone that encourages others to offer positive feedback as an end in itself.

Empower everyone

Everyone—not just leaders and managers—should be part of your culture of feedback. Here's how to make sure all voices are included:

- *Address challenges as a group.* Establish a mutual commitment among individuals and groups to work on areas that need improvement. Teach people not to fear identifying where the group is falling short—don't punish them, chastise them, or ignore their points of view—and encourage them to help one another solve problems. Feedback should be oriented toward finding solutions collectively, not dwelling on what's wrong.

- *Set clear expectations.* Make all work expectations—team and individual goals as well as ongoing assignments—clear and explicit.

Feedback should always be based on these parameters so it doesn't feel arbitrary.

- *Encourage questions.* State openly that employees should never be afraid to ask for clarification if either their work expectations or the feedback they've received are unclear.

- *Make it okay to say no.* One risk in feedback-rich cultures is that people feel obligated to say "Of course," when asked, "Can I give you some feedback?" Timing your feedback is an important part of the process. The freedom to postpone such conversations when people are not ready to have them ensures that when they do take place, all participants are willing parties.

The more you create a general climate of giving useful feedback, the more natural the process will become for everyone. That doesn't mean that you ever reach a point when you no longer have to think about it: A culture where feedback is valued is, by nature, a vigilant one. But it is the clear-eyed vigilance of a keen and progress-oriented observer, not that of a persnickety hall monitor waiting to pounce on mistakes. Engaging in active and nurturing observation—and letting others know you expect them to do the same—makes giving feedback an art that everyone you work with can appreciate.

Mastering the art of giving effective feedback takes time and careful attention. Like any skill, it is easier for some people to internalize than for others. But whether you're a feedback novice or a skilled practitioner of the craft, the specific tactics outlined throughout this book will serve as reliable touch points that you can visit again and again as you refine your style and grow more comfortable with the process.

Learn More

Quick hits

Berglas, Steven. "Don't Sugarcoat Negative Feedback." HBR
.org, September 13, 2013. http://blogs.hbr.org/2013/09/dont
-sugarcoat-negative-feedba/.
Managers can't always count on praise. Sometimes, criticism is needed to effect positive change. This piece provides tips on how to share constructive feedback most effectively.

Goleman, Daniel. "When You Criticize Someone, You Make It Harder for That Person to Change." HBR.org, December 19, 2013. http://blogs.hbr.org/2013/12/when-you-criticize
-someone-you-make-it-harder-for-them-to-change/.
It's important to focus on what needs to change, but positivity can go a long way. In this piece, Goleman argues that asking a feedback recipient about hopes, dreams, and possibilities can open him up to more effective work.

Pozen, Robert C. "The Delicate Art of Giving Feedback." HBR.org, March 28, 2013. http://blogs.hbr.org/2013/03/the
-delicate-art-of-giving-fee/.

People tend to respond most strongly to criticism. Pozen suggests the best approach to share negative feedback—and provides some tips on sharing positive feedback as well.

Books

Green, Marnie E. *Painless Performance Conversations: A Practical Approach to Critical Day-to-Day Workplace Discussions.* Hoboken, NJ: Wiley, 2013.

Most managers avoid tough performance discussions. Green helps readers conquer their fears so they can have effective feedback conversations with their direct reports. Filled with summary tips, reflection questions, conversation checkpoints, and case studies, her book helps managers find their confidence and create a workplace with a culture of accountability.

Grote, Dick. *How to Be Good at Performance Appraisals: Simple, Effective, Done Right.* Boston: Harvard Business Review Press, 2011.

This concise, hands-on guide shows you how to succeed at every task required by your company's performance appraisal and management process. Through step-by-step instructions, examples, sample dialogues, and suggested scripts, performance management expert Grote explains how to handle appraisal activities ranging from setting goals, defining job responsibilities, and coaching to providing recognition, assessing performance, and creating development plans. He also explains how to tackle other performance-management activities your company requires, such as determining compensation, developing and retaining star performers, and solving people problems.

Harvard Business School Publishing. *HBR Guide to Coaching Your Employees*. Boston: Harvard Business Review Press, 2014.

This guidebook covers the basics for coaching. The *HBR Guide to Coaching Your Employees* explains how to match an individual's skills with an organization's needs; create realistic but inspiring plans for growth; give employees feedback they'll actually apply; and provide support employees need to achieve peak performance. Readers also learn to tap employees' learning styles to make greater progress; give their employees room to grapple with problems and discover solutions; and, ultimately, keep them engaged.

Harvard Business School Publishing. *HBR Guide to Giving Effective Feedback*. Boston: Harvard Business Review Press, 2014.

Filled with actionable advice on everything from delivering on-the-spot feedback to determining if your employee is ready for a promotion, this guide—a more in-depth look at the topic of this 20-Minute Manager—provides the tools readers need to master giving effective feedback. Readers will learn how to incorporate feedback into daily interactions with employees, highlight the impact of employees' behavior on the team and the larger organization, reinforce organizational values and goals with recognition of individuals' performance, deliver constructive criticism without generating anger or defensiveness, and motivate people even when financial times are tough.

Stone, Douglas, Bruce Patton, and Sheila Heen. *Difficult Conversations: How to Discuss What Matters Most*. Second edition. New York: Penguin Books Group, 2010.

Difficult conversations can cause stress and anxiety, admit the authors of this classic—whether you need to have them with a coworker, a store clerk, or an in-law. And avoiding confrontation is not always the best option. Now in its second edition, *Difficult Conversations* shows readers how to transform tough discussions into effective learning opportunities, both inside and outside the workplace.

Weitzel, Sloan R. *Feedback That Works: How to Build and Deliver Your Message*. Greensboro, NC: Center for Creative Leadership, 2000.

In this book, leadership development expert Weitzel recommends replacing vague statements, snap judgments, and personal attacks with objective commentary that will help improve performance and change ineffective behavior using the Situation-Behavior-Impact (SBI) technique. In addition to helpful how-tos, the book includes a section of "words with impact" to use during any feedback discussion, as well as a list of dos and don'ts for giving effective feedback.

Articles

Higgins, Jamie, and Diana Smith. "The Four Myths of Feedback." *Harvard Management Update*, June 1999 (product #U9906E).

The biggest obstacle to giving constructive feedback is breaking down the myths about feedback itself. Contrary to popular belief, this article notes, defensiveness is okay, and mistakes should not be covered up or punished. Higgins and Smith provide four common misperceptions about feedback and how to overcome them to allow for more effective performance discussions.

Krattenmaker, Tom and Richard Bierck. "Is There Any Good Way to Criticize Your Coworkers?" *Harvard Management Communication Letter*, March 2000 (product #C0003F).

Criticism is a part of our work lives. It is generally viewed as negative, painful, and uncomfortable both to give and to receive. But many experts believe that giving and receiving *positive* criticism leads to continued growth. The authors of this article present tips on when and how to criticize.

Peiperl, Maury A. "Getting 360-Degree Feedback Right." *Harvard Business Review*, January 2001 (product #R0101K).

For years, Peiperl studied 360-degree feedback and asked, Under what circumstances does peer appraisal improve performance? Why does peer appraisal sometimes work well and sometimes fail? And how can executives make these programs less anxiety-provoking for participants and more productive for organizations? In this article, the author explains how executives can use purpose and scope to improve 360-degree feedback.

Phoel, Cynthia Morrison. "Feedback That Works." *Harvard Management Update*, February 2009 (product #U0902A).

Most managers say they dislike giving feedback and don't feel it has the impact it should. Those on the receiving end say they don't get enough feedback they can actually use. This article distills the wisdom of management experts into specific suggestions for creating positive and effective feedback sessions with direct reports.

Related topic: Receiving feedback

DeLong, Thomas J. "Three Questions for Effective Feedback." HBR.org, August 4, 2011. http://blogs.hbr.org/2011/08/three-questions-for-effective-feedback/.

What should I stop doing? What should I keep doing? What should I start doing? DeLong expands on these three questions that readers should ask others to get a true evaluation of themselves for better performance and growth.

Folkman, Joseph R. *The Power of Feedback: 35 Principles for Turning Feedback from Others into Personal and Professional Change*. Hoboken, NJ: Wiley, 2006.

Hearing feedback is only helpful if the recipient knows how to turn that information into change. Drawing on years of research, Folkman presents 35 principles that can maximize the value of feedback and transform it into improved performance.

Heen, Sheila and Douglas Stone. "Find the Coaching in Criticism." *Harvard Business Review*, January–February 2014 (product #R1401K).

This article focuses on making feedback more useful by teaching receivers, not just givers, how to engage in constructive feedback conversations. The authors explain why advice or assessments often don't thoroughly penetrate the receiver's consciousness, and they outline six steps to becoming a better receiver of feedback.

Sources

Primary sources for this book

Harvard Business School Publishing. *HBR Guide to Coaching Your Employees*. Boston: Harvard Business Review Press, 2013.

Harvard Business School Publishing. *HBR Guide to Giving Feedback*. Boston: Harvard Business Review Press, 2011.

Harvard Business School Publishing. *Pocket Mentor: Giving Feedback*. Boston: Harvard Business School Press, 2006.

Contributors

Argyris, Christopher, professor emeritus of education, Harvard Business School.

Armstrong, Steve, vice president, Kelly Services.

Baskette, Peter, manager, Genuity Inc.

Briggs, Anne, former product director, Harvard Business School Publishing.

Christiano, Richard, former director of facilities administration and fulfillment, Harvard Business School Publishing.

Grossman, Jack and J. Robert Parkinson, authors, *Becoming a Successful Manager*.

Harris, Jamie O., senior associate, Interaction Associates Inc.

Higgins, Jamie, senior consultant, Monitor Company.

Manzoni, Jean-François, associate professor of management, INSEAD.

Plotkin, Hal, writer and editor.

Smith, Diana, partner, Action Design.

Other sources consulted

Batista, Ed. "Building a Feedback-Rich Culture." HBR.org, December, 24, 2013. http://blogs.hbr.org/2013/12/building-a-feedback-rich-culture/.

Dolan, Cheryl and Faith Oliver. "Does Your Office Need an Intervention?" HBR.org, December 14, 2009. http://blogs.hbr.org/2009/12/does-your-office-need-an-inter/.

Gallo, Amy. "Giving a High Performer Productive Feedback." HBR.org, December 3, 2009. http://blogs.hbr.org/2009/12/giving-a-high-performer-produc/.

Molinsky, Andy. "Giving Feedback Across Cultures." HBR.org, February 15, 2013. http://blogs.hbr.org/2013/02/giving-feedback-across-cultures/.

Index

Index

respect, 7
room setup, 33

saying no, 78
scheduling, 30, 32, 67–68
self-assessment, 52–53
self-justification, 40
self-worth, sense of, 19
snap judgments, 23

talent, praising, 76
termination of employees, 51
time management, influencing, 18–19

timing, 7, 20–24
emotions and, 24
scheduling and, 30, 32
time frame for achieving
goals, 48
tone, 34
trade-offs, 65

vigilance, 29–50, 79
volatile situations, 59–64

work environment, 3–4,
73–79

Notes

Notes

Notes

Notes

Notes

Smarter than the average guide.

Harvard Business Review Guides

If you enjoyed this book and want more comprehensive guidance on essential professional skills, turn to the **HBR Guides series**. Packed with concise, practical tips from leading experts—and examples that make them easy to apply—these books help you master big work challenges with advice from the most trusted brand in business.

- Better Business Writing
- Coaching Employees
- Finance Basics for Managers
- Getting the Mentoring You Need
- Getting the Right Work Done

- Managing Stress at Work
- Managing Up and Across
- Office Politics
- Persuasive Presentations
- Project Management